Amanda Jones

The business platform

TII asbl Luxembourg
3, rue Aldringen
L – 1118 Luxembourg
Tel. +352. 46 30 351
Fax. +352. 46 21 85
e-mail: tii@tii.org
website: www.tii.org

TII - European Association for the Transfer of Technologies,
Innovation and Industrial Information:
• Founded in 1984 as a professional association.
• Currently with 300 members in 30 countries.
• Offers services in the areas of publications and meetings, networking, technology
  transfer facilitation and professional development.
• Special interest section in spin-off best practices.

THE BUSINESS PLATFORM
Entrepreneurship & management in the early stages of a firm's development
First edition 1998
Second edition 2002

ISBN 2-9599962-1-6

MAGNUS KLOFSTEN

The Business Platform

Entrepreneurship & management in the
early stages of a firm's development

Second edition

Introduction

An in-depth analysis of the factors which help to overcome the obstacles hampering the transformaton of an idea or invention into a successful business is of major importance. "The Business Platform" written by Prof. Magnus Klofsten of the Centre for Innovation and Entrepreneurship at Linköping University in Sweden is a welcome contribution to the movement to launch a vigorous, new enterprise spirit and culture for the Europe of the Third Millennium.

In the 1980s, Michael Porter described the conditions which were necessary for developing a successful business; they were commonly known as the "Porter Diamond". In this new book Magnus Klofsten analyses the factors which are vital for the launch and successful development of a technology-based firm. In future, I am sure that the "Klofsten Platform" will become a reference for studying the criteria for a firm's survival.

The UNISPIN Special Interest Section, which is part of TII, the European Association for the Transfer of Technologies, Innovation and Industrial Inforrnation, was created to encourage a greater uptake of entrepreneurial activities by higher educational institutions, and it is therefore most honoured to be associated with this study of successful business practice. Initially developed as a consortium of universities and higher educational institutions from Twente (NL), Linköping (S), Ulster (UK), Dundalk (IRL) and Catania (I) for an EC supported project, the UNISPIN SIS now operates as a European forum to network professionals involved in the establishment of spin-off companies from universities, other higher educational institutions and research centres. It promotes best practice in university spin-off schemes in regions throughout Europe and encourages entrepreneurial activity in general.

We trust that "The Business Platform" will be a helpful guide to students and researchers thinking about creating their own technology-based business as well as to confirmed SME managers and innovation consultants.

Christine Robinson
TII Secretary General

Contents

Foreword

Each year, a large number of firms are started in Sweden and abroad. In public discussions of social problems, it is often debated why more of these do not develop into medium-sized or large businesses. The answer to this question can in many cases be found in the firm's early development. My answer is because the early development in a firm is a very important phase in its life. The reasoning processes and driving forces that exist and the actions that are carried out just then can be decisive for the continued growth and development of the firm. To be able to grow in the long run, a firm must attain early on what I have chosen to call a business platform. By that, it is meant that the newly-started firm has achieved a state where vulnerability has decreased to the point that the firm has been able to move on to the next phase of its further development.

This publication is based on my doctor's thesis Tidiga utvecklingsprocesser i teknikbaserade foretag [Early development processes in technology-based firms] which was presented in 1992. Since the first version of this publication appeared in 1993, I have held a large number of seminars and lectures for a broad public both nationally and internationally. The interest for those questions that are discussed has not diminished but, rather, has intensified, and this response, in combination with the constructive viewpoints that have been put forth, has inspired me to write a new and more in-depth version for the first time in English. The target groups for this publication are entrepreneurs and persons involved in or closely connected with the process of running a business.

The theoretical model presented here is necessarily a simplification of reality, but it ought to be able to give inspiration and act as a catalyst in the furthering of a firm's development process. An important task

7

I have tried to accomplish with this book is the description of the holistic view vital in the early phases of running a business. With that, I mean that the central issue of tending the conceptual development of the firm's business activities is often accompanied by problems in areas such as administration, finance, and marketing development. By using the eight cornerstones of the development process presented in this publication, I have tried to describe this holistic view.

Many people have contributed with valuable viewpoints to the writing of this book. In this second edition, I wish particularly to thank Uno Alfredéen and Lars Malmström for their work with the new chapter «Questions and Answers». Those people who have previously influenced the contents in a constructive way are not to be forgotten, and I would like to name here Christer Angantyr, Rolf Asplund, Arne Blomberg, Kenth Ericson, Per Davidsson, Dylan Jones-Evans, Christer Olofsson, Christine Robinson, Stefan Sahlén, Börje Svensson, and Clas Wahlbin. A big thanks also to the thousands of students and business leaders who have participated in courses and seminars based on the book and who have thereby contributed to its content.

Linköping, October 2002

The Business Platform
– how you can read the book and test your firm

The business platform - another concept in the world of the entrepreneur. With the help of this book, it is my hope that you will discover that the business platform exists and that it is significant in determining how a firm will perform after the important initial phase of development following founding.

The book will also help you to analyse your firm's situation. You can with relatively good accuracy measure whether your firm has attained a business platform and, if not, get help to determine which measures ought to be taken to reach one.

The practical importance of the business platform is described with the help of three firms that have been studied while in their early phases of development.

The three firms are presented at the beginning of the book; thereafter follows a description of the fundamental problems a firm must overcome to succeed in future development.

The business platform is supported by eight important and fundamental cornerstones, as I have chosen to call them. The second part of the book describes these cornerstones and how to evaluate their strength at different levels. At the same time, you will get an insight into the practical importance of the cornerstones with the help of the three firms' stories.

In the section «What do you need to know?» three important factors in addition to the cornerstones are explained, and in the next chapter the levels on each cornerstone necessary for a business platform to be attained are described.

How each firm performed – and why – is described in the next to last section of the book.

In the final section, you can analyse your own firm. With the help of a number of questions and those answers you and other persons give to these, you can evaluate the level of each cornerstone in your firm and thereby determine whether or not a business platform has been attained.

A new chapter – «Questions and Answers» – has been added to this second edition. In it, questions often asked at seminars on the Business Platform are answered. At the end, you can analyse your own firm. With the help of a number of questions and the answers you and other people give on these, you can assess each cornerstone in the firm and, thereby, determine whether your business platform is stable or not.

Three newly-started firms

Only one will succced

Firm 1

Three young technology students from Linköping University with a burning desire to translate their knowledge into business activities start a firm. There are both driving forces and ideas. Exactly which product or products they shall decide to develop is unclear in the beginning.

After a couple of years, however, the first product has come out on the market - a system that integrated text TV and Videotex for internal and external information in places of work, in waiting rooms, in hotels, on passenger boats, etc. The market is judged to be growing.

Firm 2

The optical key was considered to be one of the best inventions of the decade. The fields of application for a key – a contact breaker – that is completely insensitive to humidity, chemicals, mechanical damage, etc., must simply be innumerable.

The optical key is, the year after its introduction, also one of the winning contributions in the invention competition SwedeInnovation.

In these circumstances, NordInvent, located in Gothenburg, founds a firm to exploit the key.

The outlook is good. There is knowledge, there is capital, and there are agreements with both Electrolux and ABB to develop the optical key.

Firm 3

Saab's aeronautics division in Linköping decides, after many years of research and development, to discontinue the development of unmanned undersea vehicles. This leads to the decision by four employees in the division, with considerable support from Saab, to start a new firm to continue the work.

The four founders of the new firm are allowed to take the prototypes of the undersea vehicles, all documentation, and a functioning network of market contacts with them. Saab also pays the salaries of the four founders during the first year of business.

Different - but good - preconditions

The three firms, Instrutec, OptiSensor, and Sutec, have different preconditions at founding. At first glance, all three appear to have exceptionally good preconditions to succeed.

But, in spite of this, only one of these firms will survive and continue to develop for a longer period of time.

Which? Yes, we will return to this. We will only reveal at this point that of the three, it is the one firm that attains a business platform which will succeed.

The Business Platform

- *a necessity for survival*

Newly-started firms are often very vulnerable. Many studies, both Swedish and foreign, show that only too many of all newly-started firms die within the first two years.

To survive and develop, a firm must reach a business platform early on. Therewith, the firm has achieved a condition where the initial vulnerabilities have been overcome, although this is not any guarantee for its future survival.

A business platform is not a goal in itself but the first, very important step towards a stable, growing firm.

What is a business platform?

The business platform model has been tested on three newly-started technology-based firms. But the model is applicable to new firms in more or less all branches.

There are also lessons to be learned, even for firms which have completely different preconditions at the beginning than those firms being studied here.

Test your firm

If you yourself have a newly-started firm, or are in any way associated with a new firm, the business platform model gives you the opportunity to pause and test your firm's situation.

Where are we on the way towards a business platform? Which parts are we good at? Which parts must be improved? These are some of the questions you can get answered by using the model to analyse your "own" firm.

The model is also applicable to those who find themselves in the planning stages or the initial phases of new business development.

Two fundamental problems

The definition of a business platform is not especially complicated. There are primarily two fundamental problems that must be solved before a business platform can be attained.

1. The flow of resources in a firm must be secured. This occurs when a sufficiently large and profitable market has been defined, when completed and accepted products are ready for the market, and when customer relations and other external relations exist in sufficient quantity and quality.

2. The firm must be able to utilise these resources; for example, by the driving force and expertise of the owners and the employees and by the development of a functioning organisational structure.

A business platform has been attained when the flow of resources is secured and the firm has the ability to utilise these resources.

14

Two sides

A business platform has both an external and an internal side. The external side means that the firm must establish relations on the market with, for example, customers, suppliers, and financiers so that requisite resources are available.

The internal side means that a sufficiently effective organisational structure must be developed so that business activities can be administered and relations established, maintained, and developed.

Capital is not the most important problem

Small businesses' supply of capital is something that is often in the spotlight. The stories of our three firms, however, show that access to capital is not the biggest problem on the road to attaining a business platform and thereby a more secure existence for the firm.

To have sufficient capital at the start does not solve all the problems. It is instead the "soft" parts in a firm's early development that must function well if the firm is to reach a business platform. Not the least among these are the development of the idea behind the firm and the definition of a market.

When has a business platform been attained?

The stories of the three firms show that it really is possible to determine when and if a business platform has been attained. If a business platform is not attained, the firm will sooner or later go under and disappear from the market. The business platform is, in this manner, a very important milestone in the firm's development. And if it is reached, it will be reached during the first two to three years, in most cases.

How well do our firms manage the fundamental problems?

We return to the stories of our firms and look at how in general they managed to solve the two fundamental problems.

INSTRUTEC

Instrutec was founded by three technology students from Linköping University. The firm was located in Linköping. The main business idea was to develop and market a system of products designed to integrate text TV and Videotex. A number of different products were developed and marketed, i.e. videocontrollers, editing terminals, graphical draw-

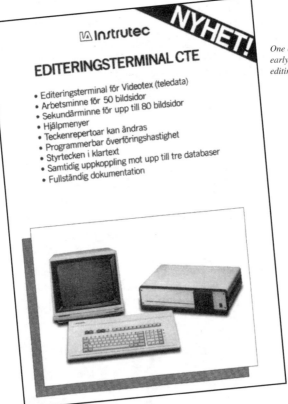

One of Instrutec's early products was the editing terminal CTE.

ing-tables, and text TV-video images. Product development occurred mainly under personal management based on the customer's system specifications. Marketing was carried out partly under personal management and partly through retail distributing agreements with Swedish, Finnish, and Dutch partners.

The firm received injections of capital at different times from a number of external sources: banks, NUTEK, Almi – the Regional Development Fund, and a few Swedish venture capital companies who had become partners in the firm. During the first five years, the firm expanded and had a peak turnover of 9 million SKr (US$1.1 million) one year. Six years after the founding, the firm employed 18 people and had a turnover of 8 million SKr (US$1 million).

Inflow of resources

The firm's development can be characterised by a cautious beginning followed by relatively strong expansion and then stagnation. The injection of resources follows largely the same pattern. At the founding, the access to resources was not especially good. Those resources which existed were the founders' knowledge, personal savings, and money from the sale of certain small services and from the premises which the county had bought and then rented out cheaply to Instrutec. The following year, an injection of resources occurred, among other things, through loans; bank credits; equipment, etc. from Philips; and revenues from the sales of the first information system.

The firm's expansion was especially strong during years 4 and 5. Sales increased and the firm received many large orders. Important relations were established with small and large customers, suppliers, retail distributors, owners, etc. On the basis of the interest that existed for the firm's products and the signals which came from different players in the market, the firm appeared to have attained a certain degree of credibility.

During year 6, this positive development ceased; sales decreased and never again reached the preceding year's level. Few new customer relations were established. Because of the stagnation, the share of resources generated from their own business activities dwindled. Seen over the entire period, the firm had difficulties generating enough revenue through sales of their own products to support their business. Liquidity crises occurred a number of times and capital was injected by the owners to secure the firm's survival.

Ability to utilise resources

From the time of founding up until year 5, Instrutec gradually upgraded their ability to manage their resources. Thereafter, no changes occurred in the firm, which either improved this ability or directly reduced it. During the first two years, the firm consisted primarily of four founders possessing a great deal of driving force and a few co-workers. All had very limited experience and knowledge of how to run a business. Fundamental functions existed, but responsibility and the division of work was fluid.

At the time of a liquidity crisis in year 3, certain changes took place that led to an improved and supplemented organisational structure. New owners, who joined the board, were able to supply expertise in certain areas which the firm had previously lacked. The new CEO who was appointed had good connections both within and outside the firm. The firm became increasingly complete in terms of the most important functions.

From year 6 on, the previously very positive development ceased. The firm no longer recruited personnel and no new expertise was added. This was because of at least two factors. The first was that a new CEO had joined the firm at the end of the year. The staff and, especially, the remaining founders had no common history with the new CEO. Another factor was that an alliance between the CEO and the external owners was formed, which created a negative atmosphere in the firm.

OPTISENSOR

OptiSensor was founded by NordInvent, a company based in Gothenburg. The idea behind the start-up of OptiSensor was to exploit the optical touch key, an invention that was one of the winning contributions to the invention competition SwedeInnovation 1981. Two products were developed and marketed. The first was a window key intended as an aid in shop-window displays, trade fairs, etc. The other was an ITD key (interactive touch display) designed as a built-in component for different types of machines, such as dishwashers, ovens, and industrial robots. Product development occurred primarily through agreements with ABB and Electrolux. Marketing was carried out under personal management and in agreement with retail distributors in the Swedish market.

New stockholder equity was injected several times from Swedish venture capital companies, NordInvent, ABB, and the 4th AP Fund. Three years after the founding, the firm employed three people and had a turnover of 0.5 million SKr (US$62,000).

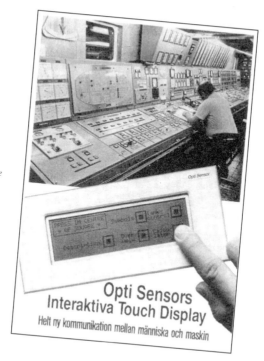

The ITD display was one of two applications for the optical touch key.

Inflow of resources

Despite backing from a strong interest group comprising two large industrial companies, four venture capital companies, development companies, etc., no business on a larger scale was generated. Access to resources was fairly good. At the founding and during subsequent development, the group of owners injected the necessary capital; moreover, the firm had access to administration, premises, network, production and product development resources, etc. It ought to be said also that relatively large amounts of resources had been invested before the founding to survey the key's technical possibilities and commercial fields of application.

What one above all hoped was that relations with ABB and Electrolux would eventually result in successful sales. Despite many years' collaboration, commercial results failed to be forthcoming, both in the collaboration with these partners as well as with others with whom the firm had relations. The revenue from sales was therefore very low or non-existent during the entire period. To run the business, the firm was in need of continual injections of capital. This took place on four occasions, the largest injection being 5 million SKr (US$625,000).

Ability to utilise resources

The firm's ability to manage resources was sufficient and fairly constant. The very simple organisational structure that existed at the time of founding was retained during the entire period of development. The founder and those closely associated with the firm possessed a great deal of driving force, were committed, and complemented each other in terms of expertise.

The idea behind the firm's structure was that administration should be kept to a minimum and that different functions should be subcontracted as much as possible. Under the circumstances, it can be questioned whether this was a good solution.

No larger problems in co-ordinating the business appear to have existed; the problems were, rather, on another level, i.e. that a strong relation of dependency on ABB and Electrolux developed. The consequences of this were experienced when Electrolux developed financial and internal problems and the contact person at ABB was transferred.

SUTEC

Sutec was founded by four people from Saab's aeronautics division in Linköping. The firm was based in Linköping. The business idea was to develop remote-controlled, unmanned undersea crafts. Many products were developed and marketed, among others, the Sea Owl, the Sea Eagle, the Sea Hawk, and the Microbe. All of the crafts were developed to carry out tasks in situations unsuitable for the use of divers. Product development in the firm was guided by the system specifications of the customers. Marketing was carried out under personal management both nationally and internationally.

The firm received financial support from NUTEK, Almi - the Regional Development Fund, Contura Mutual Fund, and the Swedish Investment Bank. The latter two have also been shareholders in the firm. Six years after the founding, the business employed 28 people and turned over 26.5 mSKr (US$3.3 million).

The "Half-Scale", that is to say the prototype of the Sea Owl, as it appeared when Sutec took over the project from Saab.

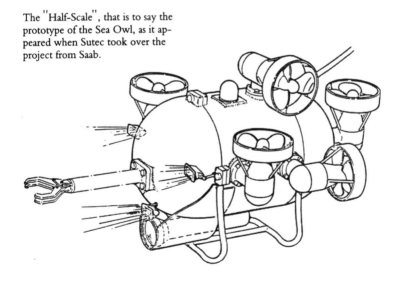

Inflow of resources

Development in the firm, characterised by a cautious start, later turned into one of steady expansion. Over time, access to resources also increased.

At its founding, resources were relatively plentiful. The most important relationship at this time was that with Saab, from which the prototype to the undersea craft, the documentation, and a functional market network were inherited. Saab also paid the founders' salaries during the first year and loaned Sutec skilled personnel when necessary. Early on, other sources of financial support were received in the form of loans from Almi - the Regional Development Fund and a few smaller orders.

At the close of the second year of business, after the first Sea Owl had been sold, the firm began to expand. The following year, relations with two large customers were established, which made up over half of the turnover during subsequent development. In combination with the fact that new customer relations were established as time went on, the firm succeeded relatively quickly in reaching a position where resources from sales made it possible to stand on its own two feet.

The injections of capital in the form of stockholder equity, credits, and loans were important supplements but probably had no decisive impact on whether the firm would attain a business platform or not.

Ability to utilise resources

The firm steadily increased its ability to manage resources throughout development. At the founding, the firm comprised four experienced founders with a great deal of driving force and who complemented each other in the areas of expertise. The organisational structure was very simple.

During year 5, the firm added new skills. New owners, who were also represented on the board, joined the firm. These supplied important supplementary expertise. Moreover, a relatively distinct structure with clearly defined areas of function and responsibility existed. The firm had 16 employees at this point.

The functional structure that existed at the founding was basically kept during the entire period of development, aside from those changes that occurred during years 6 and 7 in connection with the hiring of a new CEO and a minor reorganisation. At the end of the second year of business, the firm began more notably to increase its ability to manage resources. Among other things, the first external member of the board was recruited and the firm began to collaborate with other firms and formed a sales company in the United States. The staff increased steadily and 28 people were employed in year 8.

The cornerstones

supporting the business platform

We are therefore clear about what a business platform is – a state where the young firm has become less vulnerable and has developed stronger preconditions for future survival and development. This requires, however, that nothing dramatic occurs in the firm or its immediate environment, e.g. that a key person leaves the firm or the market slows down or completely disappears.

As can be seen in the stories of the three firms we studied, they secure an inflow of resources and manage them in different ways.

But this alone does not help those of us who would like to know exactly which factors determine if and when the business platform has been attained.

Eight cornerstones

We mentioned previously that if a business platform is attained, it occurs during the first two to three years of a firm's development. We have also seen that it is possible to determine with certainty whether or not the business platform has been attained.

Eight cornerstones, all of which must be in place, support the business platform. Each cornerstone must furthermore be sufficiently strong to hold the platform so that it does not buckle.

By studying each cornerstone and assessing its strength, it is possible to determine whether or not the business platform has been attained. But first, a presentation of the different cornerstones:

24

Four of them concern the firm's development process as such:

Note that idea and business concept are not the same thing

IDEA. *The formulation and clarfication of the idea behind the firm.* To be able to develop, the firm must have a concept from which its activities can be carried on and developed.

PRODUCT. *The development of finished products.* An essential part of the process is to develop products that are accepted by customers on the market.

Product, in this context and in the remainder of this book, comprises both products and services

MARKET. *The definition of the market.* The firm is not able to address all markets for reasons of effectiveness. One delimitation could be in terms of a niche, which is large enough to be profitable.

ORGANISATIONAL DEVELOPMENT. *Development of a functioning organisational structure.* To be able to cope with and solve problems, etc. the firm must have internal functions.

Two cornerstones concern important actors close to the firm such as the founders, the CEO, and the board members:

CORE GROUP EXPERTISE *The actors' expertise.* To found and run a firm requires different forms of expertise. If expertise in any area is lacking, active contributions of a mentor and/or input from a dedicated board of directors, for example, must be supplied.

Eight cornerstones, all of which must be in place, support the business platform.

PRIME MOVER & COMMTIMENT. *The actor's driving force and commitment.* In the early phases of development, strong driving forces and a high level of commitment by those involved in the firm are necessary.

Two additional cornerstones concern the external supply of resources in supplementary areas which are necessary for the firm:

CUSTOMER RELATIONS. *These relations are important for all firms since they are the sources of revenue.* Good customer relations are created through effective marketing and co-operation, for example, on the product development side.

OTHER FIRM RELATIONS. *A variety of different relations* are concerned here, but especially important are those that supply the firm with supplementary knowledge or financial backing.

External and internal cornerstones

Each cornerstone is more or less externally or internally oriented. The development of finished products, the definition of a market, and the establishment of customer relations and other firm relations all belong to the more externally oriented cornerstones. The more internally oriented encompass the formulation and clarification of the idea, the development of a functioning organisational structure, core group expertise, and prime mover and commitment.

Possible to measure

Now, it is not as simple as whether or not the eight cornerstones exist; rather, all eight usually exist but are developed to different degrees or are at different stages of development. For this reason, each of the cornerstones has been rated according to one of three levels, depending on how developed it is.

The high and low levels are the endpoints on a scale, where low depicts a cornerstone that is hardly or not at all developed while high depicts one that is strongly developed. The intermediate level (I) is a position in the cornerstone's development where an essential step has been taken on the path to a high level.

Thanks to these levels, it is possible to measure whether or not a firm has attained a business platform and, if not, what the firm needs to do to reach the platform.

26

Why three levels?

In this context, it can be asked why just three levels have been chosen. The reason is simply that it was not considered meaningful to use a more precise scale, that is, one with more levels.

If more precise subdivisions were made with more than three levels, the differences between the different levels would become smaller and judgements would become considerably more difficult to make.

It should, however, be pointed out that comparisons of the levels between the cornerstones ought to be made with care, since the difference between two levels differs for different cornerstones.

Cornerstone	Low level (L)	Intermediate level (I)	High level (H)	
Idea	Idea is vague. Business concept not yet articulated.	Clear, articulate understanding of the uniqueness of own products and know-how. First step towards a business concept is taken.	Business concept in initial version. It defines users (customers), their needs and ways to satisfy the latter.	*The cornerstones idea formulation & clarification, development of finished product, definition of market, and organisational development concern the firm's development process.*
Product	No finished product exists. Working model or prototype may be available.	Beta product is tested on pilot customers.	Finished product available and with key customer acceptance.	
Definition of market	Market not clearly defined. Perhaps tentative efforts to find customer categories.	Early mapping of customer categories but no priorities set.	Market basics are defined. One or more profitable niches.	
Organisational development	No organisational structure. No key functions. Informal ad hoc contacts.	Reduced overlapping of functional roles. Coordination of internal/external activities.	Operational organisational structure that enables problem-solving, incl. integration/coordination of key internal/external functions.	
Core group expertise	Necessary business and technological expertise is lacking.	Necessary business and technological expertise available.	Corporate association to actors with high and well-matched business and technological expertise.	

Cont. p 28

	Cornerstone	Low level (L)	Intermediate level (I)	High level (H)
The cornerstones core group expertise and prime mover & commitment concern important actors in the firm.	*Prime mover and commitment*	No driving force to develop a business activity. Founder(s) treat idea as a hobby.	No strong driving force to create a business activity. Small-scale commitment with personal orientation.	At least one highly committed actor striving to create a business enterprise. Strong commitment of corporate staff.
The cornerstones customer relations and other firm relations concern the external supply of resources to the firm.	*Customer relations*	Underdeveloped customer relations. Sales procedure is non existent.	Sufficient quantity and quality of customer relations. Pilot selling and sales evaluation.	Sufficient quantity and quality of customer relations. Market acceptance. Opportunity for continued sales.
	Other firm relations	No relational network for complementary resources. Shortage of capital.	No variety in other relations. Financial relations established for capital supply.	Network to supply capital, management, credibility, etc.

Cornerstone *by* cornerstone

and how our firms managed them

We have established that all eight cornerstones are necessary to build a stable (as a type of) foundation. It is important, however, to take the dynamics of the cornerstones into consideration. Which one or ones need to be developed in a given period differ from one firm to the next.

One cornerstone may not be as easy to develop as another

The cornerstones differ as to which levels have been attained, how difficult they are to develop, and how long it takes to develop them. Some of them are present at the founding. That a cornerstone is easy does not mean that it will not be a problem during development. Some cornerstones take time to develop but that does not mean that they are difficult - they simply require more time, as, for instance, in the development of a finished product and the establishment of customer relations.

That a cornerstone is difficult means that the firm is not able to develop it easily, even though both time and resources are available, for example, in the definition of a market. There is some kind of barrier which cannot be broken, or forces within or from outside the firm which obstruct development.

Four categories

The cornerstones can therefore be classified into four categories based on "entry level" and possibilities for development. Those which:
- Easily attain the intermediate level but are difficult to develop to a high level - *idea formulation & clarfication, definition of market, and organisational development.*
- Easily attain both the intermediate and high levels - *development of*

finished product, customer relations, and other firm relations.
- Already exist at the time of founding at an intermediate level and then easily attain a high level - core group expertise.
- Already exist at the time of founding at a high level - *prime mover & commitment.*

Marked differences

The three firms studied show, in many instances, large differences concerning the status of the different cornerstones at the beginning and their ability to develop them during the first three to five years. We will now describe, cornerstone by cornerstone, how the three firms succeeded.

Idea formulation & clarification

The cornerstone *idea formulation & clarification* belongs to those that are difficult to develop. Our case firms show that one can be both clear and uncertain at the time of founding about what the business should strive for.

Some have a more or less complete idea, which they had carefully thought through before the firm was founded, while others have many different ideas and make few priorities.

Overall, it takes relatively little time to formulate and clarify an idea corresponding to the first step towards a business concept (level I). It is, however, not certain whether the firm will progress further in development, i.e. that the idea will develop into a complete business concept (level H).

Instrutec's development of idea formulation & clarification
(from level L to level I)

When Instrutec was founded, there was no clear declaration of what the firm would found its activities on, either in terms of products or markets (level L). It was the founders' ambition to be business entrepreneurs; only after the actual founding did ideas begin to be generated. The generation of ideas, however, occurred very quickly and soon a number of ideas within different areas were presented.

Initially, efforts were concentrated on the development of a gauge, but after delivery was made to the customer who had ordered the project, development of such products was discontinued. Instead, another idea took hold, one that concerned information systems. This area came to constitute the basis of subsequent development. From year 2 onwards, research and development concerning products and markets for information systems was begun. By investing in this new area, Instrutec took the first step towards the development of a business concept. The following, among others, were important factors:

The period of time from the founding and one year after is designated year 1.

- There was an understanding among the founders of the uniqueness of the technique, in other words, for integrating text TV and Videotex.
- The market was judged to be in a period of strong growth and have large development potential.
- The products that were developed were customised and constituted a considerably better and simpler alternative to those of their competitors.

Instrutec, however, did not succeed in developing a business concept. There was no clear, articulated formulation of the products and markets or the business activities that would be pursued. But in any case, the firm did take the first step towards formulating a business concept (level I) sometime during year 2 (and subsequently).

OptiSensor's development of idea formulation & clarification

(from level L to level I)

The trend of events leading up to the founding of OptiSensor can be described in a number of major steps. First, it can be said that the course of events before the actual founding covered a relatively long period of time. The evaluation made the year before the founding (both regarding technique and market), indicated that the key had unique technical properties and that it was very interesting commercially. The same conclusion had been made earlier by the jury in the SwedeInnovation competition and was also made by the parties interested in being involved in OptiSensor's business. OptiSensor was founded (level L) in the light of these conclusions and expectations.

Two product ideas (the window key and the ITD key) were soon defined and from then on these came to constitute the basis of the firm's activities. From year 2 and during subsequent development, the situation could be characterised by a very good understanding of the uniqueness

31

of the key's properties and the expertise available, while at the same time great insecurity existed concerning the development of new products and markets. Large investments were made in product development and in market studies. A clear articulation of the type of business activity Instrutec intended to conduct was, however, never formulated. The firm did not succeed, therefore, in formulating a business concept (level I).

Sutec's development of idea formulation & clarification

(from level I to level H)

The founders were fairly clear from the beginning which type of activity should be pursued. This was a result of previous experience gained from the undersea technique project at Saab. The idea of starting Sutec dated from the time the founders were still employed by Saab. The trend of events leading up to the founding was characterised by the almost immediate development of undersea vehicles, which indicated that the founders had a clear idea about their firm's activities.

Thanks to the fact that Saab supplied Sutec with the prototype and the technical data as well as other forms of support, Sutec got something of a flying start. The problems that had been solved and the mistakes that had been made during the time at Saab gave the founders a clear idea of what an undersea craft should look like, which characteristics it should have, and, in general, the markets for which it was most adapted (level I).

During the first fiscal year, a business concept had been conceived in its initial version. The founders were very conscious of the unique expertise they had and how it should be translated into products. The firm had already, in principle, clearly defined its purpose and operations during the first fiscal year (level H).

Development of finished product

Firms put a great amount of time and energy into developing products. This can be one of the fundamental reasons why this cornerstone attains high levels with relative ease.

Product development has a high priority because the people in the firm are often technically minded with a great interest in developing products. Without products, there is nothing to sell. To develop a product is also more tangible than, for example, identifying a market. A finished product is something that has actually been accepted by the user and can be controlled.

Instrutec's development of finished product
(from level L to level H)
Even though a number of ideas existed one year after the founding, there was still no embryo of a product. What did exist was technical expertise, above all in one of the founders, as well as technical backup from Philips (level L). The first product was defined during year 2, but it was a very simple information system, which needed more development to be really effective. It was not a finished product (level I).

In year 3 the firm's first real product was finished, which also was accepted by many large customers (level H). From that time point, product development was primarily concentrated on improving the system and producing new ideas.

In the spring of year 4 a number of improved information systems were introduced, and somewhat later, a graphical drawing-table and a videocontroller. These were also products that had been accepted by many of the larger customers.

OptiSensor's development of finished product
(from level L to level I)
Product development occurred entirely within the framework of the agreements OptiSensor had with ABB and Electrolux. In this relationship it was Electrolux which played the privileged role. At the founding, there was no prototype or anything similar (level L).

The main purpose of the agreement with ABB was to evaluate the key for their line of products. After approximately two years of development, i.e. in year 3, there was a useable concept. Evaluation continued, however, for one more year and, in spite of the fact that the

33

key had not been successfully adapted to any product, the previous agreement was extended in the fall of year 4. The following spring, the co-operation was dissolved because the contact person at ABB had moved, and not because an application had not been found. The agreement with ABB therefore did not lead to any commercial exploitation of the key.

The co-operation with Electrolux was more fruitful than the cooperation with ABB. Product development actually took place in three parallel processes (development of the window key, adaptation of the ITD key to the white goods line of products, and development of the ITD key for more general applications).

The window key was finished and delivered for the first time in the spring of year 3. In the fall of the same year, the first ITD key was delivered to a customer. It was difficult to find acceptance for the products. The window key did not function satisfactorily, and the customers found it difficult to operate. The ITD keys that were sold had more the character of trial samples.

In the fall of year 3 a prototype of the ITD key for the white goods line was delivered. Even though it did not function particularly well, it was thought that it would be ready to use within the near future. The earlier agreement was therefore extended, as it was in the previous case, at the end of year 4, but no product was actually finished.

In the spring of year 5, the firm still did not have a finished product, that was accepted by important reference customers. What existed were two products, which were tested by a number of users and which were sold to a very limited extent (level I).

Sutec's development of finished product
(from level L to level H)
Initial product development at Sutec was primarily oriented towards using the ideas they already had and modifying the prototype of the so-called Half-Scale, the undersea vehicle designed by Saab (level L). After little more than a year and a half, the first Sea Owl was finished and delivered to a customer (level I). During the following year, more Sea Owls were developed for different customers. Apart from the Sea Dog project (formerly the Sub), which after a few years was discontinued, product development became more and more concentrated on the development of different versions of the Sea Owl.

Consequently, Sutec had a finished product on the market at an early stage. From the time that the first Sea Owl had been delivered, less than two years passed before it had been accepted by many large reference customers (level H). The situation was the same for the other versions which were developed.

Definition of market

Definition of market, similar to idea formulation & clarfication, is a cornerstone that has proved difficult to develop. Firms initially find it easy to acquire relevant customer categories (level I) but thereafter find it difficult to prioritise and define a profitable market (level H). Their actions can be likened to bids, which have no priorities, or chances and opportunities that turn up on the market.

Why are the cornerstones *idea formulation & clarification* and *definition of market* difficult to develop? One explanation is that a sort of "self-awareness" is necessary to be able to develop them, i.e. an ability to see possibilities on the market, customers' needs and desires - and be able to exploit them within the firm's current context. They are also difficult, because they are abstract and difficult to concretise.

At the company's founding, it is therefore simpler to proceed from a solution based on one's own constructed problem rather than to proceed from someone else's problem and then try to solve that. The cornerstones are therefore easy to develop up to the intermediate level.

To go further means that the firm has been clearly accepted as a supplier by the market. It is not so strange that these cornerstones are difficult to construct. Even if their characteristics are different, they have a lot in common. The distance between a business concept and its market is short, and as such these cornerstones partially overlap each other.

Instrutec's development of definition of market
(from level L to level I)
In the beginning, Instrutec was primarily occupied with two parallel activities. The first was an evaluation of the different information systems already on the market. The aim was to find out which problems these systems solved but, above all, which problems they could not solve (level L). The second was a market survey where a number of customer segments, the number of possible users within these segments, and the competition on the market were defined.

In the fall of year 2, the founders were clear about the fact that they should develop tailor-made solutions and that these should be marketed to customers in shops, hotels, and offices, among others. They had, on a basic level, sieved out a few categories of customers, but no direct priorities between these were made. During development, the firm did not succeed in finding a niche, which was sufficiently large to be profitable. Although a market share of 70% - 80% was attained in two of the three market segments that were worked up, the revenues generated were insufficient (level I).

OptiSensor's development of definition of market
(from level L to level I)
The firm put much energy into studying and analysing the market. To some extent, this had been done before the company was founded. The work, however, was aimed more at developing applications and in general studying the commercial potential. Directly after founding, marketing work became primarily concentrated around two activities.

The first was to evaluate those product ideas the firm already had and market demand. Much work, in particular, was put into the ITD key to define its advantages over existing key systems. The second was to try to define relevant customers, calculate sales potential, and map the extent of the competition for both the window key and the ITD key (level L).

36

In the case of the ITD key, the customers were judged, above all, to be large firms. It was hoped that the key would be used by ABB and Electrolux. These were already large potential users at the time of the founding and were judged to be OptiSensor's large markets. As for the ITD key's general applications, OptiSensor never went beyond defining a number of potential users. Accordingly, it can be said that OptiSensor managed to pinpoint a number of categories of customers during year 2. But a niche that was sufficiently large to be profitable was not identified (level I).

Sutec's development of definition of market
(from level I to level H)
During the time at Saab, much work had been put into investigating and surveying the market for undersea craft. This was documented in various written reports. Much indicated that the market was in a period of strong growth. When Sutec was founded, this valuable documentation was then released to the founders. An essential part of the marketing work in the beginning was therefore to go through and analyse this documentation so that it could be used to the greatest possible extent for the current ideas. At the same time, new market surveys were conducted to update and supplement the earlier material (level I).

This easy access to market information and the superior knowledge that existed made it possible for Sutec, as early as year 1, to identify a market which encompassed both the civil and the military offshore sectors. The competition was hard, but because of the vehicle's special characteristics, the possibilities to offer customers tailor-made vehicles, and the great expertise that existed, Sutec had a sufficiently large and profitable niche (level H).

The market Sutec intended to address was world-wide. The firm was very active on the market, mainly by way of personal visits. The first presentation of the Sea Owl took place in the United Stated one year after founding. During year 6, a difference of opinion developed over priorities to be given to the civil and the military markets. But no change in the concentration of marketing efforts was made.

Organisational development

The organisational structure of firms is designed in a way to be expected in small, young firms, i.e. simple, flexible, and informal. A functioning organisation is usually not found in the beginning (level L), but one that consists of important functions such as finance, marketing, and production is soon developed (level I). It is therefore usually sufficient for the business being conducted at this stage.

Sometimes it is diffficult to develop an organisational structure to a high level because there are forces within the firm that resist the formation of formal structures. A functioning organisation encompasses effective management of internal and external problems and relatively well-defined roles and functions. Entrepreneurs do not always want this. They prefer a structure that allows for flexibility and creativity. Another explanation can be that it is difficult to create stability in a young firm, because of conflicts between the different players in the firm. It can be complicated to form a suitable constellation of players that is beneficial for the firm's growth and development.

Instrutec's organisational development
(from level L to level I)

During its development, Instrutec never had more than 18 employees. Throughout its lifetime it remained a small firm and kept a simple organisational structure with basic functions. From the time of founding and for the next two years, the founders and another two staff were the only ones active in the firm. Even though a certain division of functions had been made, the lines of responsibility were vague and who would do what was variable (level L). A change in the structure soon occurred.

The most radical change took place during year 3 and was caused, above all, by two events. The founder, who was also the CEO, left the company. The firm also had a liquidity crisis.

The change meant that the firm was reorganised to a certain extent and that an external CEO was recruited. New owners joined the firm and also became members of the board. At the same time, the marketing organisation was reviewed. During the year, more staff were recruited for the firm.

Seen from an organisational standpoint, the change was positive since the firm now, to a considerably higher degree than previously, had a functioning organisational structure. This meant that work could be structured better, that the division of work was more clear, and that external and internal activities were somewhat better co-ordinated (level I). One additional change was made in year 6. It was not as comprehensive as that in year 3 although the consequences had greater impact. In principle, the change meant that a new CEO was recruited and that a review and a certain reconstruction of the marketing operation took place. On the whole, the organisational structure remained unchanged.

During development, it was difficult to create stability in the business and avoid liquidity crises. The collaboration between the board and the firm could also have been better. In spite of this, the firm could be said to have had a structure that was sufficient for managing resources.

OptiSensor's organisational development
(already level I at the beginning)

OptiSensor had a very simple organisational structure divided into internal and external functions. It was sufficiently good to be able to manage resources (level I).

The internal functions basically consisted of a CEO, owners and a board of directors. At most, three people were employed in the firm. External functions were product development and production, which were managed by an agreement with Electrolux. The work performed by OptiSensor was mainly marketing, certain administrative tasks, and cultivating relations that had been established. During the development phase, two large changes occurred in the organisation.

The first happened in the spring of year 4 when the CEO resigned. At the same time, two of the owners, who were also board members, left the firm. One year later, another change occurred in the ownership and the board, but which led to no large structural changes in the firm. The functions were the same as at the founding, but the people involved were in some cases new.

Was the organisational model, which was implemented from the outset at OptiSensor, appropriate? Much indicates that there was a structure which reduced overlapping between different functions and which made a realistic co-ordination of external and internal activities possible. No structure corresponding to level H, however, was developed.

Sutec's organisational development

(from level L to level H)

On the basis of the expertise possessed by each of the founders, a division of functions was made: finance, marketing, technical development, production, and system technique. The organisational structure was consequently very simple with basic functions. Even though a division into different functional areas had been made, responsibility was nevertheless fluid (level L).

Soon, a number of major changes occurred:

- Sales companies were formed in the United States (year 2) and in Great Britain (year 5) to be closer to international customers.
- New owners joined the company (in the fall of year 2 and the spring of year 5) which gave the firm a more complete board.
- Multiplane was acquired (in the spring of year 6) and Swemac, a subsidiary, was formed.

Up through year 6, the firm basically had the same division of functions, which existed at its founding. The staff that was recruited conformed to the existing organisational structure. Above all, the technical side of the organisation expanded while marketing was still more or less managed by the CEO. In the spring of year 7, the CEO was replaced, and at this

40

time (and in this connection), a minor change was made in the firm. A number of new functions such as project development, quality control, and client service were introduced.

At its height, Sutec had 28 employees, and throughout the period covered it kept a simple organisational structure. It should also be mentioned that initially people were "on loan" from Saab.

Little by little, a structure emerged, which in a fairly effective manner made a coordination between internal and external activities possible. A certain amount of understaffing existed on the marketing side, but external board representatives supplemented this to a certain extent.

The conclusion is that from the end of year 1 the firm had a suffficiently effective organisational structure for the business being carried out (level I). Another upgrading of the organisational structure took place (level H) in year 5 when new owners joined the firm.

Core group expertise

Access to expertise in firms is usually good. At their founding, level I and, in certain instances, level H have usually been attained. The founders and other actors closely involved in a firm are highly educated and in many cases have long professional experience in relevant areas. It is often the case that many company founders complement each other in terms of expertise. If expertise is lacking, it is acquired by recruiting a competent board.

Coregroup expertise is a cornerstone that exists at the time of founding for many reasons, primarily because the firm was started for the purpose of exploiting an expertise. It constitutes a sort of natural resource, which exists thanks to the founders and other actors closely involved with the firm. Another reason, which can be seen from the above, is that expertise, if it is needed, is relatively easy to acquire, for example, through different partners.

Instrutec's development of core group expertise

(from level I to level H)

During the first two years, core group expertise in the firm was primarily to be found in the founders. Since it was a young team of founders, they had very limited experience of working life and of running a business. Technical knowledge, which they had acquired during their studies at university, was in ample supply. Knowledge of finance, marketing, sales, organisation, etc. was limited to one of the founders and was of a more theoretical nature. But the core group expertise present was relevant to the actual situation (level I).

Organisational changes in year 3 added expertise within many important areas to the firm. It came primarily from venture capital companies, and it was mainly a question of expertise coupled with experience.

In venture capital companies, there were people who, through their work on the board, supplied experience from earlier positions in industry and experience of starting and running firms. As for the managing directors, the level of their expertise and experience was similar to that of the founders, apart from somewhat more work experience.

From year 3 on there was clearly expertise within and associated with the firm that must be considered to have been relevant and sufficient for the business. There were actors with high levels of expertise, who also complemented each other with business skills and technical proficiency (level H).

OptiSensor's development of core group expertise

(already level H at the beginning)

The access to core group expertise was very good during the entire period of development. Those closely involved with the firm had a high level of both technical and business education, experience from different positions in industry and, in a few cases, also experience in starting and running a firm.

Those associated with the firm complemented each other in terms of expertise. The technical knowledge was found, above all, in the founders but also in NordInvent, the industrial firms, and the first CEO. Marketing expertise was found primarily in the managing directors. All of the partners had good experience from different positions in industry.

Experience in running a firm was found mainly in NordInvent and the venture capital companies. The latter also had experience in starting firms. Consequently, a number of important actors with a high level of expertise as well as business professionalism and technical knowledge were involved in the firm (level H).

Sutec's development of core group expertise
(from level I to level H)
The founders mainly had a technical education and only one of them did not have an engineering degree. All had working experience (in some cases long) but none or very little experience in running a business (level I).

The external owners who became involved with the firm from year 2 on supplied the expertise that was lacking in the founding group, i.e. primarily financial expertise but also experience in starting and running a business. Especially from year 5, when the Swedish Investment Bank and Contura Mutual Fund were represented on the board, the mixture of expertise in the firm was good.

During the firm's development, access to expertise was consequently good. It is true that the founders lacked experience in running a firm, but their backgrounds in industry, on the other hand, were varied. They also complemented each other in technical and marketing expertise. Although only one of them possessed the latter, it was of a very high level. The core group expertise in the firm was further strengthened by the expertise of the external board members (level H).

Prime mover & commitment

Development is promoted by people with a strong driving force and great commitment to the business. This is true not only for founders but also for the other actors closely involved with the firm. It is understandable that this cornerstone is well established from the start because it is a precondition for a firm to be founded and be able to develop at all. The cornerstone is, as can be seen, the most fundamental and must be found in all firms intending to progress rapidly.

Instrutec's prime moving forces & commitment
(already level H at the beginning)

Even though the founders each had different personalities and backgrounds, the driving forces behind the start of the firm were the same for the whole group. They wanted to start and run a firm. During the first years, the activities of the firm were very wide. Ideas were thought up, products were developed, marketing information was collected, and relations were established with different partners in the market.

The driving force and strong commitment were not affected by the changes that took place in the course of year 3. The new CEO who was recruited had a very positive effect and was very popular, both within and outside the firm. He was even deeply engaged in the firm's activities. Venture capital companies that entered the firm at the same time were also strongly committed to the business. They were, of course, interested in the firm growing and in their invested capital growing.

From its founding onwards, there were consequently one or more individuals who had a strong commitment to building up a firm. There was also, during the same time period, a high level of commitment in general (level H).

OptiSensor's prime moving forces & commitment
(already level H at the beginning)
The driving force behind the start of OptiSensor was the desire to commercialise the optical key and to build up a firm around this using a model created by NordInvent. The business was characterised, especially during the early years, by a strong driving force and a deep commitment on the part of those involved.

NordInvent was the prime mover, and in a tangible way exercised a dominating role within the firm. Relations were established and resources were created by NordInvent. The managing directors felt that NordInvent interfered too much, which was also the reason why they left the firm. Other actors (managing directors, industrial firms, venture capital companies, etc.) were not nearly so dominating, even though they had invested capital and were interested in making a return on it. During the development phase, there were therefore many actors with a strong driving force to build up a firm and, in addition, a high level of commitment (level H).

Sutec's prime moving forces & commitment
(already level H at the beginning)
There were, above all, two driving forces that were behind Sutec's founding: first, the desire to realise personal ideas; second, a high level of dissatisfaction with working in a large firm. Sutec was a firm dominated by the founders during its development and strongly influenced by the founders' driving force.

The CEO was an especially strong prime mover and was also the most important force behind the founding of the firm. Compared with the founders, the other actors involved were not at all as dominating.

The firm's development was marked by a strong commitment of those involved, which was reflected in the active product and market development. There was also a desire to build a firm (level H).

Customer relations

When a firm is founded, there are no established customer relations (level L). Relations are, however, established successively (level I, until finally the quantity and quality of customer relations are sufficient (level H). The cornerstone is easy to develop since it has a high priority, as does the cornerstone *development of finished products*. The establishment of customer relations is considered to be one of the fundamental cornerstones in a business. Without customers, the firm will not survive in the long run. Another reason is that the cornerstone is very concrete. It is possible to measure how many customer relations there are and how much they contribute. When a customer relationship is established, something tangible occurs.

Instrutec's customer relations

(from level L to level H)

The firm established a number of different customer relations during development, both with final customers (12) and with retail distributors (6). The following can be said about the firm's customer relations:

- From the time of founding and for the next year, a total of three relations were established. The sales were small but they were important since they were the first sales and acted as references for the firm. In year 2, four new relations were established, both with retail distributors and final customers. The first export deals were carried out by Salora and Wärtsilä.
- The first large sales were made during year 4 to the Royal Viking Hotel and to Tidningarnas Telegrambyrå (TT).
- In year 5 most of the customer relations were established (a total of 6). Half of them were relations with retail distributors. From year 6 to the spring of year 8 only three new relations were established.

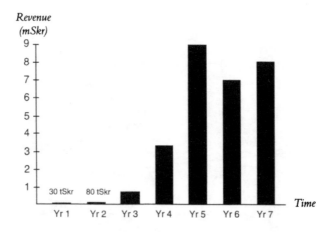

Accrued revenues – Instrutec

Both the number of relations and accrued revenues increased from year 1 through year 5. In year 6, the number of relations was the same as the year before, but accrued revenues decreased. Thereafter, the number of relations decreased while the revenues increased slightly from the previous year. It is therefore difficult to say anything about the quality of the relations in general from the above data. Instead, the individual relations must be discussed.

Seen over the entire time period, over half (10) of the relationships were of a short-term character and lasted a maximum of one year. Among these were four retail distributors, of which all but one (Nova Vision) sold very little. Of the end users, two (Teledata Utveckling and Luftfartsverket) could be considered to be relatively large.

Those retail distributors who sold well were Teledatorer and City Com. The customer relationship with Teledatorer lasted the longest. The reason it ended in 1986 was that Teledatorer developed financial difficulties. Instrutec lost a very important customer when the collaboration with Teledatorer ceased. Moreover, the firm no longer had a retail distributor in the Swedish market.

Those end users who can be considered to be the largest and most important were Royal Viking Hotel and Tidningarnas Telegrambyrå. Orders from these companies gave Instrutec a foothold in the market, which demonstrated that many important customers accepted the information system. Thereafter, three more relations were established with large customers: Televerket Kable-TV and Volvo in year 5 and Stjärn-TV in year 6.

With the above as a starting point, the following factors can be emphasised as to the quantity and quality of the customer relationships:
- From year 3 to year 5, 12 of a total of 18 relationships were established. The firm had established relationships with two important retail distributors and many large end-user groups. The turnover increased greatly during this period.
- From year 6 on, few new relations were established. Relations with both the retail distributors and end-user groups still existed. However, the firm's turnover decreased.

To summarise, at the time of its founding, the situation was at level L, and after a little more than a year, level I had been reached. From year 3 on, the relations established were such that the firm had been accepted by many large customers as a distributor (level H).

OptiSensor's customer relations

(from level L to level I)

At its founding, there were no customer relations, but during the firm's subsequent development, four customer relations were established, of which two were with retail distributors and two with end-user groups. The first relation was established during year 3 with a retail distributing agreement with Owells. After a short time, however, the relationship ceased and only a few window keys had been sold by the distributor.

The next year, the ITD key was sold to FFV Aerotech. In addition, a retail distribution agreement was signed with Nordqvist & Berg for the ITD key. Both of these companies were the customers with which OptiSensor had the longest standing relations. During the same year, a consignment of window keys was also sold to Luxor.

What can be seen from the chart below is that the customer relations that had been established did not generate any considerable revenue. Even though three customer relations had been established in year 4 and the buyers were large companies and organisations such as FFV, Luxor, and Nordqvist & Berg, the quantities ordered were very modest. The firm's turnover therefore did not exceed 0.5 million SKr (US$62,000).

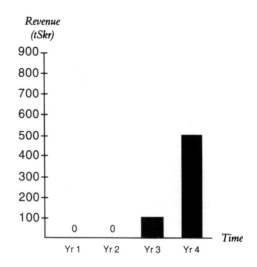

Accrued revenues – OptiSensor

The sales that were made were entirely in the form of samples or for the purpose of evaluation by the customers. In conclusion, OptiSensor began at level L and attained level I after little more than a year.

Sutec's customer relations

(From level L to level H)

A total of eight customer relations were established during development and all were with end-user groups. The firm did not have any established customer relations at the outset. In the case of Sveriges Television and SUDO Import, it was a question of smaller deliveries of components, but as first customers, they were still important. As for Bergen UW Services, Wärtsilä, and ABB, it was a matter of large, one-off deliveries of Sea Owls. The largest customers were the Swedish Marine, Stolt Nielsen Seaway, and Hallstrom. The first delivery of the Sea Owl took place in the fall of year 2 and from year 3 on there were important customers both in the national and the international markets.

Also characteristic of development was that the number of customer relations per year was relatively small (at the least one and at the most four) but that the revenues increased sharply during these years.

The Swedish Marine and Stolt Nielsen Seaway were particularly large customers, above all in year 7. They were responsible (from year 3 on) for a little more than half of the firm's revenues generated each year.

Judging from the above, it seems to be that Sutec started out at level L, attained level I a little more than a year and a half later, and somewhat later (at the end of year 2 or the beginning of year 3) established a sufficient quantity and quality of customer relations (level H). During the entire development, in principle, there were at least two large customers which regularly placed orders. Important references existed, which also increased the chance of sales to new customers.

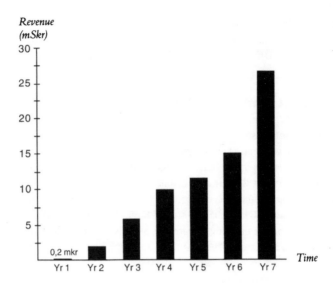

Accrued revenues – Sutec.

Other firm relations

The cornerstone other firm relations belongs to those that are easy to develop. One important part in a firm's business activities is the establishment of financial relations. The range of such relations is wide, consisting of venture capital companies, development companies, and banks, among others. On the whole, access to financial resources is good (level H). Many relations (besides customer relations) have the characteristic of being strategic. Usually it is a question of large companies, where relations are of a technical nature or where there are different owners.

One explanation why other firm relations are easy to develop depends on the nature of the cornerstone. Relations with financiers can be established without there being any finished product or before the market has been defined. What is necessary is credibility, so that financiers feel reasonably sure that they will not only be able to recover their invested capital but make a profit as well.

Another example of why this cornerstone is easy to develop is the relationships with suppliers. Here, it is the supplier who has the commercial

52

interest. Why should he say no to a business proposition? As with the development of finished products and customer relations, this cornerstone, with the characteristics described above, is concrete.

Instrutec's other firm relations

(from level L to level H)

In addition to customer relations, 13 other relations of different types were established. Over half (8) of the relations were of a financial character. Included here were actors such as Handelsbanken, the Swedish Investment Bank, NUTEK, Almi - the Regional Development Fund, and Wermlandsbanken, whose only contributions were injections of capital. Another group in this area consisted of ProVex, VenCap, and Nordic Venture who, because of their commitment as owners, participated in the everyday work of the board and in this manner also contributed management expertise.

The remaining relations consisted of the suppliers SATT Elektronik and Svensk Elektronik, Loewe-agenturen, Linköping County, and Philips. At the time of founding or soon after, two relations were established that meant that the firm, among other things, had access to low-cost premises. The most important relationship was the one with Philips from which essential backing was obtained during the early development of the information system. From year 2 to year 4, a large share (7) of the relations were established. Here, it was a question of different forms of capital injection and supplier relations.

During year 5 and later on, four new relations were established when Wermlandsbanken took over Handelsbanken's banking commitment. Nordic Venture took over VenCap's share. NUTEK granted loans and Loewe allowed the firm to be an agency for one of their terminals.

During the firm's development there was no lack of relations - above all on the financial side. At its founding, however, Instrutec was at level L and after little more than a year on level I. It is difficult to judge to what extent the firm had access to the capital it needed. It is, however, clear that when liquidity crises occurred, enough capital was injected so that the crises were soon resolved. From year 3 on the firm had a relatively large variety of other relations (level H).

OptiSensor's other firm relations
(already level H at the beginning)
The number of other firm relations established was considerably greater than the number of customer relations. A total of 12 relations were established, of which 8 constituted some form of financial involvement. Another aspect is that, of all the relations established, 8 were established at the time of its founding.

What is also striking is that almost all of the relations that existed at the beginning continued throughout the entire development. In principle, it was only Ventura and VenTech who after a little more than two years left the firm and ABB who discontinued their collaboration in the spring of year 5.

Those relations that were established after its founding were with Götabanken, from whom the firm received credit; Arbit and Philips, with whom the firm for a short period received help in developing software for the window key; and the 4th AP Fund, from whom the firm received capital in year 5 and who became a new owner in the firm.

During its development phase OptiSensor had access to a great many different resources through their relations with industrial companies, venture capital companies, institutional investors, and development companies. It was a matter not only of capital but also of resources such as production, product development, and management support from the board of directors. There was therefore a rich variety of relations from the beginning, which gave the firm important supplementary resources, i.e. level H at the time of founding.

Sutec's other firm relations

(from level I to level H)

During its development stage, a number of other relations were also established. A total of 11 relations with different actors such as financiers, product development partners, and those who offered more general support to the firm were established.

The fact that the founders were able to acquire the prototype, etc. to the Half-Scale very advantageously, could borrow personnel, and received a year's salary each made Saab a very important relation early on and one which was more or less active during the entire period of development. Year 2 was the year when most of the firm's relations were established.

Four of them, Almi - the Regional Development Fund, NUTEK, the Swedish Investment Bank, and SE-Banken, were purely financial. The Sea Dog project was initiated with Kockums and Scantech (who also became shareholders in Sutec).

During years 5 and 6, a number of important events affected these relations. The first was that the earlier projects and collaboration with Kockums and Scantech were discontinued. During these years, the Swedish Investment Bank and Contura Mutual Fund joined Sutec as owners and members of the board. Together with Thorn EMI Electronics, Sutec conducted advanced discussions on a mutual project for product development; however nothing came of them. The following year, contacts with Saab were intensified when the Multiplane was acquired. In addition, relations with ABB Oil & Gas and with SIND were established through the project "Havsindustriell Kompetensutveckling [Development of Sea Industry Expertise]".

With the above relations, Sutec acquired a number of important supplementary resources. At its founding, Sutec was at level I, above all thanks to its relations with Saab. In the beginning, it was mainly a question of financing or financial support. With time, resources in the form of management were also made available. In addition, Sutec participated in a number of research & development projects, which increased the firm's credibility in the market; i.e. level H was attained after little more than one year.

What do you need to know?

We have determined that some cornerstones are more difficult to develop than others. There are three additional characteristics that are important to consider:

- The time of founding is a very important factor. The firm's status at founding as far as the level of the cornerstones is concerned is a good indicator as to its subsequent development.
- The first three years, and especially the first two, are a very intensive part of the firm's development. Thereafter, development of the cornerstones diminishes substantially.
- There seems to be some sort of latching effect concerning the development of the cornerstones. None of the cornerstones in any of the three cases studied slipped back to a relatively lower level.

The firm's status at the time of founding is important

The situation at the time of founding is interesting for many reasons. One key reason is that those cornerstones that are initially developed to a certain level at the start strongly affect the firm's future development. Some firms are founded without any large amount of preparation. Others are founded after many years of planning and activities. Those firms whose founding was preceded by preliminary activities developed the cornerstones furthest.

The firms studied have a common factor in that, at the time of founding, they had developed many cornerstones to levels that are not especially difficult to attain, even if the cornerstones in general were poorly developed. Those cornerstones that are the most developed in all three firms at the time of founding are *core group expertise and other firm relations.*

56

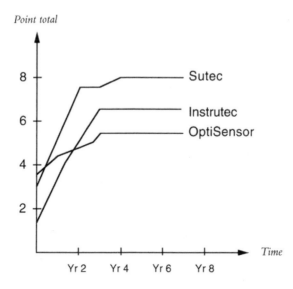

Point total

An overall picture of a firm's situation in terms of the development of the cornerstones can be obtained by assigning points to the different levels. Here, a low level has been given 0, an intermediate level 0.5, and a high level 1 point, after which the points were added at different time points. Since the different cornerstones cannot compensate for each other, this is not a wholly accurate construction. At the same time, though, it illustrates well three important observations:

1. The level of the cornerstones' development at the beginning is important. OptiSensor has a high total at the start, but the wrong cornerstones were developed, causing the firm to achieve the lowest sum of points after three years.
2. The greatest development occurs during the first two years. Thereafter, no pronounced development occurs.
3. There is a latching effect, which means that the levels that have been attained are not easily lost.

But there are also large differences between the three firms which have a direct correlation with the fact that they prepared for the start of their firms in different ways and had different preconditions at founding. The most significant difference is that the firms were at different levels in the development of the more difficult cornerstones: *idea formulation & clarification* and *definition of market*. This is the difference, which later is revealed to be significant for attaining a business platform.

Preliminary activities

A firm that already at the beginning has developed the difficult cornerstones, idea formulation clarification and definition of market, have greater chances of attaining a business platform

It appears to be that if the difficult cornerstones, primarily *idea formulation & clarification* and *definition of market*, are relatively strong at the time of founding, a business platform will probably be attained. To have a strong *definition of market* cornerstone also means that the weaker cornerstones will gradually come up to speed.

The firm's status at the time of founding is therefore important and is a good indicator for subsequent development. When founding is preceded by preliminary activities, correspondingly more cornerstones will be highly developed.

It is, however, very important to determine which cornerstones are developed. *A firm that has many highly developed cornerstones does not automatically mean that future development will be without problems. The right cornerstones must be developed.*

The firm's development during the first years

After three years, no development of the cornerstones appears to occur. A firm which has not attained a business plaform by this time runs a large risk of going under, even if it takes time-as much as ten years.

Apart from isolated liquidity crises, the firms studied here had no great problems surviving the first two years. It is, however, apparent that a strong development of the cornerstones occurs during the first years (especially the first two). It is also apparent that development of the cornerstones stagnates after three years. Further development of the cornerstones after the three first years is the exception.

After the first three years, it can be established that firms are in different positions. Some are less vulnerable since they have achieved a business platform, while others are still vulnerable. Any further development of the cornerstones that reduces vulnerability does not occur after the first three years. Those firms whose development stagnates continue to be as vulnerable as they were during the third year.

There is, therefore, nothing that defines a general time point or limit, where the firm's vulnerability decreases. But there is a palpable risk *that if a business platform is not attained during the first three years, the firm may continue to be vulnerable and finally go under.*

Firms that attain a business platform manage future development well, while those who do not attain a business platform remain vulnerable and eventually go bankrupt, are closed, or are reorganised. The latter process can take a long time, in some cases up to ten years.

Why three years?

Why does the development of the cornerstones begin to stagnate after approximately three years? One reason is that an ability to develop the difficult cornerstones is lacking. This can be traced to the founding and the insight into the business which is to be run. *To understand the term business platform and the cornerstones which support it gives a much better starting point for future development.*

If most of the difficult cornerstones have already been solved, either in part or completely at the time of founding, the firm will also succeed in fully developing them to a high level.

Idea formulation & clarification and definition of market are critical

In those firms where the cornerstones *idea formulation & clarification* and *definition of market* have only been vaguely developed at the time of founding, any subsequent development of these cornerstones will be incomplete. Despite this, it is still possible for the firm to develop finished products and establish a sufficient quantity and quality of customer relations.

The difference between a vulnerable and a less vulnerable firm appears, at first sight, not to be particularly large in terms of the number of levels attained with respect to the different cornerstones. *What is most interesting, however, is not the number of levels attained but, rather, which cornerstones are developed.*

The latching effect

Another observation in these cases is that something similar to a *latching effect* in the development of the cornerstones appears to exist. If a certain level has been attained, the firm will not sink to a lower level as long as nothing dramatic occurs. This is true, regardless of whether it is level I or level H that has been attained.

One explanation for this phenomenon can be that when a cornerstone is developed to a higher level, the level of expertise and experience in the firm has also been increased.

Greater insight

If the firm, for example, has succeeded in defining its market, this means that the firm has acquired greater insight. This insight is not easily lost, if nothing dramatic occurs. The same can, for example, be valid for the development of a functioning organisational structure.

When certain structures have been developed and they have been seen to work well, there is no reason to make the situation worse. The firm recognises what works well and will see that it remains so.

The business platform

what levels are necessary for attaining one?

So far, it is clear that a business platform is a necessity for the firm that is to have a chance to prosper and develop. It is just as clear that there are eight cornerstones supporting the business platform.

But what do the different levels imply; must one be the best in everything to survive?

No, not the best, but good. This means that a high level must be attained on some of the cornerstones while an intermediate level on others is sufficient.

Idea

Level I must be attained. To be able to grow and develop, a firm must have an idea, which determines its direction. It is therefore important that the idea is made clear so that the unique expertise which is the basis of the firm's business is really understood and can be communicated both within and outside the firm. When this happens, the first step has been taken towards a business concept, which is necessary for a business platform to be attained. A full-fledged business concept, however, is unnecessary.

Product

Level H must be attained. A product is something that satisfies the needs and desires of customers. If a product is lacking, the firm then has nothing to offer. After a product has been defined, it is a matter of getting it accepted by one or more reference customers. When this happens, the firm has shown that it can produce something that is accepted by others - that it is capable of satisfying needs and desires on the market.

Market

Level H must be attained. To define a market means that the firm must clarify which customers it intends to conduct business with. It is not enough to chose a few customer categories, which simply seem to be interesting. The firm must go one step further and define a market, that is sufficiently large and profitable. If the firm succeeds in the task of defining a market, there will be enough available resources, which make growth and development possible.

Organisational development

Level I must be attained. To be able to conduct business, the firm must develop an organisational structure, which facilitates the co-ordination of activities. This structure ought to be formed so that flexibility and creativity are utilised, external relations are maintained in a somewhat effective manner, and co-ordination of the internal work is possible. A formal organisational structure is unnecessary - an informal one that works sufficiently well is adequate.

Core group expertise

Level I must be attained. In the firm, both technical and business expertise is necessary to be able to develop products and markets. Access to high-level expertise, however, is not a goal in itself. A high level of expertise is necessarily needed to attain a business platform. The important thing is that the expertise is relevant to the situation.

Prime mover & commitment

Level H must be attained. One basic requirement for a firm to develop is that there is at least one person with a strong driving force and a through and through strong commitment by the others closely involved with the firm. A firm that has no prime mover or commitment of this type will not be able to carry out changes and activities which are necessary for a business platform to be attained.

Customer relations

Level H must be attained. Without customer relations, the firm will not be supplied with the revenues necessary for its development. It is not enough that occasional sales take place to different customers; there must be sufficient quantity and quality of customer relations. If this is the case, the firm will receive resources they have generated themselves, and it will be accepted by its customers as a reliable supplier.

Other firm relations

Level I must be attained. This type of relation complements the cornerstone *customer relations.* In some situations the firm will need to be supplied with capital, management expertise, and other forms of resources as a "lubricant" in their business activities. A great variety is not necessary - but it is essential that the firm has access to the requisite capital.

To be able to attain a business platform, the firm must achieve at least level I on all the cornerstones. Four of the cornerstones, of which three are more externally oriented, must also be developed to level H.

The cornerstones cannot compensate for each other

An important question on a more general level is whether it is possible for the strongly developed cornerstones to compensate for the weaker ones. For example, whether a poorly defined market can be compensated by finished products or whether weak driving forces can be compensated by well-developed ideas or vice versa.

All the cornerstones must be developed to the indicated level. If a cornerstone is underdeveloped, it cannot be compensated by another that is stronger than is necessary.

The answer is an unequivocal no. Compensation between the cornerstones is never possible. The cornerstones each constitute important parts of a whole, which must exist if the firm is to survive and develop.

What happened to the firms

- a comparison

Instrutec

Instrutec was close to attaining a business platform but never quite reached one. The firm was actually as close to attaining a business platform as was possible. There was only one cornerstone left to develop - definition of a market.

The supply of resources increased intensively during an expansion period. In the firm's third year, revenues were 3.4 million SKr (US$425,000) and the year after 9 million SKr (US$1.1 million). Thereafter development stagnated.

An important reason is that Instrutec did not succeed in defining a market or a niche, which was large enough to be profitable. This is best shown by the fact that although the firm relatively quickly became the market leader with their information system, the market was not large enough to generate sufficient resources for the firm.

We noted earlier that a lack of preliminary activities gives a lower value rating for the firm's subsequent survival. Instrutec is an example of this. When the firm was founded, there was no clear concept of what the activities should be based on. The difficult cornerstones *definition of market* and *idea formulation & clarification* were only on level L when the firm was founded.

What happened afterwards?

Instrutec faced recurring liquidity problems, not least because the firm had difficulties generating sufficient resources through sales.

In the fall of year 8, Instrutec again had a serious liquidity crisis. Instrutec tried to solve the problem and conducted discussions with venture capital companies and other possible financiers. After a short time, contact was made with Industrifonden, who decided to inject capital with the stipulation that the external partners, i.e. the venture capital companies, should match their investment.

Negotiations lagged and a solution was never reached. One of the main reasons was that one of the venture capital companies had large problems with other commitments and could therefore not afford to invest more capital in Instrutec.

Instrutec tried to solve the problem with a number of business transactions designed to accommodate profit transferral. The firm would, for example, buy another firm which had a large surplus and then sell the inventory of the firm they had bought.

Such measures, however, were no solution, only a way to make things more difficult for themselves. The following year they were forced to buy everything back at a higher price than the amount it would have cost to produce everything themselves.

After encountering a number of difficulties in the search for solutions, ProVex suggested that Instrutec merge with Cosmos Parabolteknik in Kristinehamn, which was a firm owned in part by ProVex.

Bankruptcy

The personnel at Instrutec, however, emphatically turned down the proposition since it meant moving from Linköping. There was now only one solution - to declare Instrutec bankrupt.

After bankruptcy, Instrutec's assets were acquired by Registrator Industri AB in Karlstad, who also became the staff's new employer. One of Instrutec's founders became the firm's new CEO.

Registrator had a large order from ATG Trav och Galopp, and Registrator thought they needed the expertise which Instrutec possessed to be able to complete the order. Registrator did not consider the purchase of Instrutec to be an acquisition but rather a merger. The staff at Instrutec would be able to remain in Linköping.

Problems soon arose in the relations between the new owners and the personnel from Instrutec. Despite attempts to solve the problems, the situation finally became intolerable.

Instrutec's personnel tried to buy back the "old firm", but Registrator refused. This resulted in the personnel resigning from Registrator at the beginning of year 10 and forming a new firm, PS Presentation System Inc.

Examples of what Instrutec could have done

As mentioned above, it was the cornerstone *definition of market* that was not adequately developed so that a business platform could be attained. At its founding, Instrutec began at level L but managed to develop this cornerstone to level I after approximately one year: that is, the firm had sifted out customer categories relevant to their products. They had not, however, made any priorities among their customer categories nor analysed where the profitable customers could be found.

They could, therefore, have put more effort into defining their market. The divisions the firm made, Videotex, hotel, etc. were not good. Instead, they should have tried to find other principles for division, which would have yielded a larger market potential There was marketing expertise, both in the firm and in the vicinity, which could have been more effectively utilised for this.

OptiSensor

OptiSensor did not attain a business platform and was not even close to achieving one. The firm made appreciable sales but did not generate enough resources. The business was supported by the owners injecting capital into the firm on repeated occasions - during the life of the firm approximately 10 million SKr (US$1.25 million) were pumped into the firm.

It is not difficult to point out which cornerstones OptiSensor failed to develop far enough. In the first place, the firm never succeeded in producing a product that was accepted by a customer. Those deliveries that were made of the ITD key were not more than trial samples for evaluation.

As for definition of market, OptiSensor never did more than sift out the relevant customer categories. No priorities were ever made, perhaps mainly because the product was not fully developed and therefore never had any clear area of application.

What happened afterwards?

In the spring of year 8 a new CEO was recruited (the third since the founding) by OptiSensor. The new CEO only worked part-time for the firm, which continued to be confronted with problems.

Sales deviated greatly from the budget and only a few window keys and ITD keys were sold.

Nordqvist & Berg, on whom large expectations had been placed, had great difficulties selling any ITD keys. After a time, Incentive (the main owner of Nordqvist & Berg) decided to merge Nordqvist & Berg with another firm. Reductions were made and the ITD key was removed from the line of products.

In the spring of year 9, financial problems occurred in Electrolux. The person in Electrolux Mecatronik responsible for contacts with OptiSensor resigned. At the same time, Electrolux replaced the entire management at Electrolux Mecatronic and collaboration with OptiSensor ceased.

The new CEO had begun to develop a new application for the optical key during his time at OptiSensor. "Guided Waves" was the name of the new concept and a prototype was ready in the late fall of year 9. Much work was put into development and market surveys. NordInvent actively sought financing from NUTEK and Almi - the Regional Development Fund - but was turned down.

A conflict between NordInvent and the new CEO developed over how the work on the project should continue; this led to his leaving OptiSensor at the end of year 9.

One of the main people in NordInvent was recruited to be OptiSensor's fourth CEO. During the tenth year, a gradual reduction in the activities of OptiSensor was begun. Further external financing was out of the question.

A few ITD keys were sold to old customers, but this income could not support the firm. The new CEO was transferred to other duties in NordInvent, and the business was closed down.

The optical key was put in mothballs. The inventor of the key took back the rights and began a collaboration with Philips with plans to use the key in ceramic stove togs.

Examples of what OptiSensor could have done

OptiSensor therefore did not succeed in attaining an adequately high level on the cornerstones *definition of market, development of finished product, and customer relations.* Two other cornerstones, *idea formulation & clarification* and *organisational development* were also poorly developed but did reach the level necessary for a business platform.

To some extent, the failure to develop products can be blamed on unfortunate circumstances such as the departure of the person at Electrolux who was OptiSensor's contact. The same thing happened in the collaboration with ABB when OptiSensor's contact was offered a new job abroad. The collaboration with these two customers/collaboration partners therefore came to nothing.

OptiSensor ought to have had closer ties to both Electrolux and ABB where there were clear applications for the ITD key. If they had succeeded in getting one of these firms to use their products, the outcome would probably have been a different one.

The question is also if it was correct to work with the window key and the ITD key in parallel. The window key proved early on to have a series of problems that made it difficult to find acceptance on the market. A more pronounced emphasis on finding a field of application for the ITD key would perhaps have been necessary.

Sutec

Sutec clearly attained a business platform. The firm succeeded in generating enough resources to be able to stand on its own two feet, at the same time as it developed an ability to manage resources. During development, some new capital was injected, but the firm was not dependent on this for its existence.

It is also interesting to note that, thanks to the ongoing development of the Sea Owl project at Saab, Sutec had already developed two of the more "difficult" cornerstones, *idea formulation & clarification* and *definition of market*, to level I. One year later, these had been developed to level H.

What happened afterwards?

In year 8 the earlier positive development changed at Sutec. Development came instead to be characterised by financial problems and reductions in personnel, above all during years 9 and 10.

The turnover sank in year 8 to 21.3 million SKr (US$2.7 million), the following year to 13 million SKr (US$1.6 million), and in year 10 reached only 15.9 million SKr (US$2 million). The number of employees decreased from 28 to 20 during this period. In year 10, the firm suffered a loss of 3.4 million SKr (US$0.43 million).

This downturn in business for Sutec can primarily be attributed to a slow market for the products.

In the fall of year 8 Multiplane was sold to Trustor, a firm owned by the chairman of the board. Investments were made in the AROV project initiated a few years previously and in those ideas already discussed for the Sea Twin.

The firm was also engaged in other projects. These included a development project with Norwegian partners. This project, however, was discontinued in year 9 since the financing expected from the Swedish Norwegian Industrial Fund (SNIF) was not forthcoming. Another project was the so-called Super SubSea, but this project was also discontinued in year 9 because of the altogether too large commercial uncertainty.

At the same time, a prototype for the Sea Twin was completed, tested and presented to the military and civil markets. The AROV project was completed and a report delivered to FMV for evaluation. The project had still not resulted in any products, but it was hoped that on the basis of the investigatory work, FMV would place some orders with Sutec. At about the same time, development of a new version of the Sea Owl, the Sea Owl 500, was begun and completed the following year.

The firm continued to be active in both the civil and the military sectors. Potential customers, both in Sweden and abroad, were visited and exhibitions were made at trade fairs.

Weak flow of orders

Despite all efforts, the flow of orders remained weak and the market appeared to be uncertain. The offshore market was weak and was not expected to expand until the oil price stabilised at a higher level. Government defence policies were not favourable for Sutec either, and the most important customer, the Swedish Naval Forces, had set new priorities and were very reserved in placing new orders.

During year 9, Sutec received financial support to the sum of 4.75 million SKr (US$590,000) via a directed new emission to Scantech A/S in Norway and Charterhouse Bank in the United Kingdom.

New owners

In the fall of year 10, Bofors Underwater Systems acquired all of the stocks and options in Sutec.

Bofors' involvement in Sutec was perceived as very positive, both by the employees and by the market. Sutec now had a strong owner and Bofors Underwater Systems now had a civilian product under their wing. Torpedverkstaden had for a number of years had their own Sea Owl for trial shooting activities in Vättern [a lake in south-central Sweden].

Thanks to the change in ownership, glimmers of hope for an increase in demand began to appear, and Sutec's order book began to grow again.

Similarities *and* differences

between the firms

Cornerstone	INSTRUTEC "almost"	OPTISENSOR "not at all"	SUTEC "definitely"
IDEA *Level I* *necessary*	At the founding, L, but after less than 1 year, I. (No well thought through idea at the founding. The first step towards a business concept was taken but the firm went no further.)	At the founding, L, but after half a year, I. (No well thought through idea at the founding. The first step towards a business concept was quickly taken, but the firm went no further.)	At the founding, I, and after 1 year, H. (A well thought through idea at the founding and a quick development of the business concept.)
PRODUCT *Level H necessary*	At the founding, L. After 1 year, I and a half year later, H. (No finished products at the founding. Concentration on a strong concept. Many finished products were developed over time.)	At the founding, L and after 1.5 years, I. (No finished products at the founding. Unclear about product development. No finished products were produced.)	At the founding, L. After 1.5 years, I and half a year later, H. (No finished products at the founding. Concentration on a strong concept. Many finished products developed over time.)
MARKET *Level H* *necessary*	At the founding, L, and after less than 1 year, I. (At the founding, the firm was un-	At the founding, L, but after little more than 1 year, I. (At the founding, the firm was un-	At the founding, I, and after little more than 1 year, H. (At the founding, the firm was clear

Cornerstone	INSTRUTEC "almost"	OPTISENSOR "not at all"	SUTEC "definitely"
	clear about the market. After a time, it knew which market was interesting. No profitable market was defined.)	clear about the market. After a time, it knew which market was interesting. No profitable market was defined.)	about which market was interesting. A profitable market was quickly defined.)
ORGANISATIONAL DEVELOPMENT *Level I necessary*	At the founding, L, and after 2 years, I. (No functioning organisational structure at the founding. After a time, it became adequate. No effective functioning organisation was developed.)	At the founding, I. (At the founding, the organisational structure sufficed. No effective functioning organisation was developed.)	At the founding, L. After little more than 1 year, I, and 3 years later, H. (No functioning organisational structure at the founding. Soon it became adequate. After a relatively long time, a high level of experience was developed.
CORE GROUP EXPERTISE *Level I necessary*	At the founding, I and after 2 years, H. (At the founding, there was sufficient expertise for the situation. After some time, there was a high level of expertise.)	At the founding, H. (During the entire development, there was access to a high level of expertise.)	At the founding, I, and after 1 year, H. (At the founding, there was sufficient expertise for the situation. After a relatively long time, there was a high level of expertise.
PRIME MOVER & COMMITMENT *Level H necessary*	At the founding, H. (During the entire development, there were strong driving forces and a strong commitment.)	At the founding, H. (During the entire development, there was access to a high level of expertise.)	At the founding, H. (During the entire development, there were strong driving forces and a strong commitment.)

Cornerstone	INSTRUTEC "almost"	OPTISENSOR "not at all"	SUTEC "definitely"
CUSTOMER RELATIONS *Level H necessary*	At the founding, L. After 1 year, I, and 1.5 years later, H. (No customer relations at the founding. After a time, a few were established. Later, there were a sufficient quantity and quality of customer relations.	At the founding, L, and after 2.5 years, I. (No customer relations at the founding. After a time, a few were established, but a sufficient quantity and quality of customer relations were not established.)	At the founding, L. After 1.5 years, I, and a half year later, H. (No customer relations at the founding. After a time, a few were established. Shortly after, there was a sufficient quantity and quality of customer relations.)
OTHER FIRM RELATIONS *Level I necessary*	At the founding, L. After 1 year, I and 1.5 years later, H. (No important other firm relations existed at the founding. Soon, a few were established. After some time they multiplied.)	At the founding, H. (During the firm's entire development, there were multiple relations.)	At the founding, I, and after 1 year, H. (Important other firm relations existed at the founding. After some time, they multiplied.)

Consolidating

the business platform

We have tried to show in this publication what is necessary for a firm to attain a business platform. Early development is a very important period in a firm's life. During the first two to three years, the foundation for future development is laid. If the firm overcomes its early vulnerability and thereby attains a business platform, the chances for survival and continued development are increased considerably.

We have shown that it is fully possible to determine if a firm has attained a business platform. If that is not the case, it is possible to determine how much is left to achieve on each cornerstone and, at the same time, to point out a number of measures that must be taken for a business platform to be attained.

It is important to emphasise that one must not take things for granted after a business platform has been reached. Naturally, it is a goal that means that an important stage in the firm's development has been successfully passed - but there are many problems to solve, even after a business platform has been attained. Remember, also, that it is possible to slip off the business platform. It is therefore worthwhile tending the platform while at the same time proceeding with the further development of the firm.

In conclusion, we hope that you have found this publication interesting. Consider it as a handbook where comparisons with help of the cornerstones and development in the three firms that are described give a clear picture, which will make the diagnosis of deficiencies in a firm and the possible measures for correcting them easier.

Questions & answers

This chapter examines the questions that have been asked most frequently about the Business Platform in different kinds of seminars – both national and international. It takes the form of a discussion that took place between the author and the entrepreneur Uno Alfredéen.

What is the difference between drawing up a business plan and using the Business Platform model?

A business plan expresses the firm's ambitions, it describes the firm's goals and is as such a kind of prognosis. The Business Platform is an analytical tool that is used to describe where in the business plan the firm is right now and as such is a kind of diagnostic instrument. The business plan maps the firm's journey into the future. The Business Platform offers a situational analysis that indicates which point the firm has reached on that journey. It can be used as a check list and, if needed, as a guide to revise the business plan, and it also provides a basis on which to perform the so-called SWOT analysis (Strengths, Weaknesses, Opportunities, Threats). This can be used when situations arise in the firm that require an important decision.

At the same time it is important to understand that a business platform analysis is partly a subjective assessment of soft factors. The result is dependent on who performs the analysis, and if it is to be used to help make comparisons between firms, the analyses should be made by the same person or group. While the business plan ought to be a more comprehensive and well elaborated document that requires time and resources, it is possible early on and relatively simply to make an analysis with the Business Platform model. Such an analysis also narrows down the discussion to the most important issues, i.e. the firm's weak points.

What relevance does the Business Platform have in the so-called New Economy?

Nowadays we can say that the 'New Economy', if anything, is a digitalised version of the old. It has not brought about any new ways for building a business. The principles behind successful firms are still the same, such as customer benefit, return on equity, and job satisfaction. At one time, many thought that new firms could be created without addressing the customers' wishes and without giving shareholders adequate return on invested capital. Experience has shown, however, that there are no shortcuts – the cornerstones of the Business Platform must be developed to grow quality firms. The Business Platform is based on the traditional rules of the game. Had this model been used on the IT firms that were part of the new economy, they would most likely have changed their business plans as time went by.

Are there other platforms that can be used by young firms?

The following new platforms have been suggested:

- the Start Platform (before). Used before the firm is started. The Start Platform is the stage when a business idea appears to be commercially viable and the entrepreneurs make the transition from merely discussing and studying the idea to active business development. The goal is to make the firm survive.
- The Due-Diligence Platform (after). The firm is ready to be quoted on the Stock Exchange (if that is the goal) or to open up the capital to outsiders and must meet the requirements of an initial public offering.

Why are traditional business ratios not adequate to portray a true and fair picture?

The traditional business ratios are insufficient to assess newly-started, fast-growing firms. On the other hand, all young firms will reach a stage where traditional business ratios are relevant. In certain stages of growth, these firms have such strong dynamics that traditional business ratios do not suffice to paint a true and fair picture of the firm's current situation. Above all, these firms lack a stable history. As a result it becomes impossible to make comparisons over time. This does not imply that all traditional business ratios are misleading. The least meaningful is usually the attempt to measure solidity.

Cash flow analyses, on the other hand, should be made for all firms from day one. Other business ratios that can be relevant for these firms are customer acceptance, the use of rolling financial plans instead of a budget, measures of cash expenditure in the firm, or any combination of these. Regardless of whether any of these business ratios are used or if units of measure are formulated, the measurements must be made in real time and on a regular basis.

Basically, there are two ways to measure a firm: the statistical method and the dynamic method. The Business Platform is a dynamic method that measures soft factors in a precise manner. It can be combined in an advantageous way with other models that rate knowledge. In certain phases of a company's development, it can also provide more relevant information than traditional business ratios. The Business Platform should be seen as a tool box and the final result depends on who is using it.

How are measurements made?

Analyses made according to the platform model are subjective assessments of soft factors. There are no predetermined values for the freezing or boiling points of young growth businesses. A good way to improve precision is to let those with more experience do the analysis.

Can the model be used with all types of firms?

Yes, in principle, but the analysis is most meaningful in the early stages of a firm's development, before the firm has stabilised. The relevance of a business platform analysis depends more on the firm's position on the development curve than on what type of firm it is or its size. The Business Platform can be used to supplement the so-called SWOT analysis, which is applicable to all firms. In certain cases, this also applies to the systems of subsidiary companies. For them, it is important to be aware that, as subsidiaries, they do not own their balance sheets or their strategies, which is why some of the tools in the Business Platform lack relevance.

In practice, there are two different ways to use the model. It can be used to create a holistic view or to serve as a basis for discussion. It makes it easier to focus on the questions that are most relevant for the firm at a given time. It helps create a common view among different people and levels in the firm. The analysis can also be used to track how well the firm is following its business plan. For young entrepreneurs, this is a natural attitude. For venture capitalists, it is a way to assess the firm and revise its business plan in a structured way.

How should the Business Platform be used and by whom?

For the board of directors and management of a firm, the Business Platform is an instrument for checking that the right things are done at the right time. For the entrepreneur, it is a relevant basis for discussion in meetings with his or her mentor. For venture capital companies and investors, the Business Platform can be used to analyse the firm from the aspect of capital procurement and to check and revise its business plan.

How important is capital?

Capital procurement is often the main concern for young growth businesses. But capital procurement is only one of the eight cornerstones of the Business Platform. The study of our three firms also revealed that access to capital is not the biggest problem in the attempt to attain a business platform. Access to capital is important, but other cornerstones, such as the market, are at least as important, if not more.

An idea without capital has a greater chance of survival than capital without an idea. Many successful firms have grown organically without any big injections of external capital. An external supply of capital that is overly generous does not always encourage the right behaviour in the firm, while a limited and regulated supply usually promotes good management of its assets. An analysis using the Business Platform model is an instrument that guides investors on how to allocate financial support to businesses. It signals when and how goals should be met or adjusted.

Why are idea and marketing issues often difficult for entrepreneurs?

Both idea and market are abstract terms which are difficult to define. One problem is that most entrepreneurs begin with the product – not the market – and therefore do not interpret customer needs correctly. Pioneering technical innovations usually arise when an entrepreneur has an idea for a solution to a technical problem, and subsequently, attempts to find clients. It is first when you reverse the process and reshape the idea according to real customer advantage that the idea becomes a business idea. A market that is sufficiently large to support the firm must be defined.

Too few business leaders/entrepreneurs have the ability and/or resources to reshape their ideas according to the customers' demands and needs. And without clients, no business can succeed – however good the idea is. Developing a product in collaboration with a customer is one way to dramatically shorten the road to an economically sound business platform. It is even better if the customer can be persuaded to participate in funding the development of the product. Such clients exist and have already let themselves be convinced. It would take a lot for them to choose another solution than the one they themselves have participated in developing.

Learning to modify and reshape an idea according to the customers' demands and needs is a mental process that naturally leads to product development. By understanding that the customer, and nobody else, ends up paying the salaries, is often a profitable way of looking at things.

Test your firm

How far has your firm progressed in its development of a business platform? With a knowledge of the contributing factors, i.e. cornerstones, which are necessary to build up a business platform, it is possible to determine if you have succeeded in attaining one. And if not, how far is left to go.

Above all, an analysis increases insight into which measures are necessary to attain a business platform.

Using the "test questionnaire" on the following pages, you can determine which possible concrete measures are necessary for those cornerstones which your firm has perhaps not developed as far as is necessary.

To facilitate your evaluation, it is recommended that you go back to those sections that concern the cornerstones' different levels. On the opposite page, you will see examples of how the "test questionnaire" can be used. A one-year-old firm, HYC (Hide Your Computer), who analyses the cornerstone *idea formulation & clarification* will, after reading this book and using the evaluation tables on page 82, decide that their business concept has attained level I. A number of measures have then been suggested which should allow the firm to reach level H.

If there are not enough lines for your and others' evaluations, use a separate sheet of paper.

NERSTONE	TASK	MY EVALUATION
a el which must reached: **1** OUR LEVEL: **1**	1. How did the idea for the firm originate?	1. Mine — 8 years ago.
	2. How is the business concept communicated within the firm?	2. Planning meetings 1X/mo.
		3. Marketing materials, customer visits by sales representatives.
	3. How is the business concept communicated externally?	4. Salesmen are able to argue for the uniqueness of our product.
	4. Do the firm's employees have a clear understanding about which idea(s) are the central ones? Describe how.	5. Need — reduced risk of computer theft. Who — small, computer-intensive firms.
		6. The concept works.
	5. Which customer needs ... ll be satisfied and	7. Not the cheapest, but the most ...cily used and the most effective up

ANOTHER INTERNAL PERSON'S EVALUATION	EXTERNAL PERSON'S EVALUATION	THINGS TO DO
1. Lasse's innovation.	1. Lasse Larsson's idea.	
2. Meetings now and then.	2. — — —	2. Meetings more often with an agenda.
3. Brochure and customer visits.	3. a 4-page brochure and direct sales.	3. Design a marketing plan.
4. There is only one product. Most realise the possibilities with it.	4. So far, only one idea. Supplementary products in the same niche are necessary in the future.	4. Formulate a business concept which includes the development of more products in the same niche.
5. Fear of computer theft and loss of data in the firm.	5. The need of small- and medium-sized firms to not let the human factor (forgetfulness, sloppiness) cause computer thefts.	5. Define the customer group more specifically.
Risk for computer theft ...reases greatly, which is ...y to show.	6. Eliminate the human factor.	
...ery effective, but ...nsive.	7. An expensive solution which works.	
...r product works.	8. Need is there. The first deliveries ...	

Testing form

CORNERSTONE	TASK	MY EVALUATION

Idea
Level which must
be reached: **I**

YOUR LEVEL:

....

1. How did the idea for
   the firm originate?

2. How is the business
   concept
   communicated,
   internally and
   externally?

3. Which customer needs
   are to be satisfied and
   how?

4. Do the firm's
   employees have a
   clear understanding of
   which idea(s) are the
   central ones?

5. What is it that makes
   the firm's business
   concept a business
   opportunity?

6. Describe the
   uniqueness of the
   concept in relation to
   those of your
   competitors.

ANOTHER INTERNAL PERSON'S EVALUATION	EXTERNAL PERSON'S EVALUATION	THINGS TO DO

Testing form

Product
Level which must
be reached: **H**

YOUR LEVEL:

....

1. Describe the status in product or concept development – do you take into account customers' input?

2. Is there any important reference customer ready to verify the product's utility?

3. What is it that made the firm choose to develop just this product?

4. Is there anything which indicates that the firm has been accepted as a reliable supplier? If so, in what way?

5. Is it appropriate to seek a patent or other intellectual property rights for the product or concept?

84

ANOTHER INTERNAL PERSON'S EVALUATION	EXTERNAL PERSON'S EVALUATION	THINGS TO DO

Testing form

CORNERSTONE	TASK	MY EVALUATION

Market
Level which must
be reached: **H**

YOUR LEVEL:

....

1. Describe the firm's
method of developing
its market. Does the
firm develop its
market in a structured
manner, e.g. by its
own personnel,
representatives, or
built-in customers
(e.g. OEM
customers)?

2. What characterises the
segment or the niche
that the firm is
addressing?

3. What criteria are there
for the choice of
market segment or
niche?

4. Describe in what way
the firm
communicates with its
current or potential
clients.

5. Does the firm intend
to develop its clients
vertically (clients in
the same industrial
sector or with the
same business logic)
or horizontally (offers
to clients outside the
sector)?

86

ANOTHER INTERNAL PERSON'S EVALUATION	EXTERNAL PERSON'S EVALUATION	THINGS TO DO

Testing form

6. Describe the advantages for the customer, or the customer segment or niche, which the firm supplies.

7. How will the customer segment or niche develop further and thus allow the firm to grow (through focused offers to more customers or a broader range of products)?

Organisation
Level which must be reached: **I**

YOUR LEVEL:

....

1. Describe the firm's current organization, both the formal one and how it works in practice.

2. Is the organisation tailored to the firm's business processes – is it, for example guided by what the clients think or by product/technical factors?

ANOTHER INTERNAL PERSON'S EVALUATION	EXTERNAL PERSON'S EVALUATION	THINGS TO DO

Testing form

3. How are tasks delegated to the staff, and how independently are they able to work? How is responsibility shared? Has an order of delegation been developed? How do you distribute work and solve problems?

4. Describe the organisation's "threshold" and "ideal weight" – i.e. how much larger can it become before more fundamental changes become necessary, before efficiency in satisfying customers is lost and working conditions become difficult?

ANOTHER INTERNAL PERSON'S EVALUATION	EXTERNAL PERSON'S EVALUATION	THINGS TO DO

Testing form

CORNERSTONE	TASK	MY EVALUATION

Core group expertise
Level which must be reached: **I**

YOUR LEVEL:

....

1. What are the firm's main sources of expertise and where is it located?

2. Describe the business expertise that exists in the firm, for example, in terms of business judgment, marketing, and sales.

3. Describe what experience of leadership exists in the firm and how relevant it is.

4. Is there access to previous business experience?

5. Describe what experience the firm has in problem-solving.

6. What kind of important expertise is missing in the firm?

7. Do the members of the board contribute to the firm and how?

8. Is there a system that reduces the risk of "brain drain" (bonus, ownership, and so on)?

ANOTHER INTERNAL PERSON'S EVALUATION	EXTERNAL PERSON'S EVALUATION	THINGS TO DO

Testing form

CORNERSTONE	TASK	MY EVALUATION

Prime mover & commitment
Level which must be reached: **H**

YOUR LEVEL:

....

1. Why was the firm started?

2. Who or what is the «motor» in the firm?

3. What are the motives for continuing to run the business today?

4. How would you describe the staff's motivation and commitment to the firm – the firm's atmosphere?

5. Describe the differences in opinion that exist over how the firm's activities should be run.

Customer Relations
Level which must be reached: **H**

YOUR LEVEL:

....

1. Describe the contacts that the firm has with its customers.

2. How many clients does the firm have and what is the percentage breakdown of each of the four largest?

3. Describe to what degree the firm has regular customers.

94

ANOTHER INTERNAL PERSON'S EVALUATION	EXTERNAL PERSON'S EVALUATION	THINGS TO DO

Testing form

4. What are the most important common reactions by customers, for example, during pilot sales?

5. How are customer complaints handled? Describe.

6. How are customers and the follow-up market handled? Describe.

7. What is the potential of existing customers and of possible new customers? (Can the business be "scaled up"?)

8. What should the firm do so that more clients will choose the firm as a supplier?

ANOTHER INTERNAL PERSON'S EVALUATION	EXTERNAL PERSON'S EVALUATION	THINGS TO DO

Testing form

CORNERSTONE	TASK	MY EVALUATION

Other firm relations

Level which must be reached: **I**

YOUR LEVEL:

....

1. What kind of relations does the firm have besides customer relations (for example, financial, technical, and legal)?

2. How is the firm securing its supply of expertise?

3. Has the firm had problems getting support from external supporting actors necessary for the firm's development?

4. Describe how the firm is open to the external business world (i.e. positive to alliances and networking)?

ANOTHER INTERNAL PERSON'S EVALUATION	EXTERNAL PERSON'S EVALUATION	THINGS TO DO

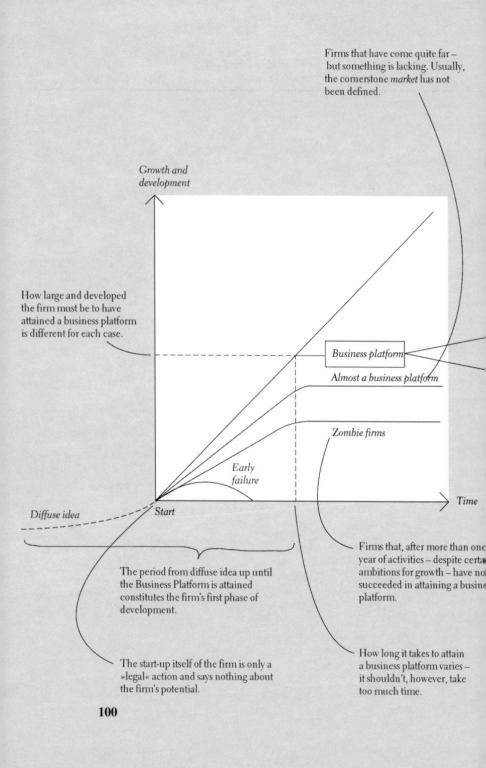

Firms that have come quite far – but something is lacking. Usually, the cornerstone *market* has not been defined.

Growth and development

How large and developed the firm must be to have attained a business platform is different for each case.

Business platform

Almost a business platform

Zombie firms

Early failure

Time

Diffuse idea

Start

The period from diffuse idea up until the Business Platform is attained constitutes the firm's first phase of development.

Firms that, after more than one year of activities – despite certain ambitions for growth – have not succeeded in attaining a business platform.

The start-up itself of the firm is only a »legal« action and says nothing about the firm's potential.

How long it takes to attain a business platform varies – it shouldn't, however, take too much time.

100

CORNER STONES   LEVELS

                                    L   I   H

┌─────────────┐
│ Attracting │   ──── Idea   ────   ────   ────
│ resources   │
└─────────────┘
                              Product   ────   ────   ────

                              Market   ────   ────   ────

┌─────────────┐   Organisational development ────   ────   ────
│ Managing   │
│ resources   │
└─────────────┘   Core group expertise ────   ────   ────

                              Prime mover & commitment ────   ────   ────

                              Customer relations ────   ────   ────

                         ──── Other firm relations ────   ────   ────

101

An experienced businessman/entrepreneur's view of the business platform

>> I see the Business Platform model primarily as a valuable method specific to the problems of young firms in the early stages of business development. My experience has shown that early development in firms is often not just a marathon race but principally a relay race. Frequently a change must occur in leadership style, corporate structure, choice of role in the business network, financial actors, and customer offers.

The model provides a practical, usable system, both in terms of deciding the firm's status and degree of business maturity as well as in terms of guiding and managing the firm's subsequent development.

The model is a good help when, for example, it concerns identifying critical events and important secondary goals for the firm's business activities. Both the serial and simultaneous interactions between external events in a firm's customer milieu and surroundings, and the internal organisational structure undergoing strong growth, are more easily managed. The model makes possible structured thought in boards of directors, leadership groups, advisory boards, and similar bodies.

Furthermore, in the communication of often complex conditions and relationships, the model offers a common nomenclature which can be applied in the same way by the many different parties involved within and around a firm in its early/critical phase of development."

UNO ALFREDÉEN

Learning Resources
Centre